CHESTER TO WARRINGTON

Vic Mitchell and Keith Smith

MP Middleton Press

Front cover: Smartly presented, 4-6-0 no. 45647 Sturdee *roars over Mickle Trafford junction with the 09.15 Leeds to Llandudno express on 20th August 1966. (H.Ballantyne)*

Back cover upper: Railway Clearing House junction diagram for 1903 for the Chester area.

Back cover lower: The 14.23 Chester to Liverpool was worked by no. 142060 on 13th May 1997 and is seen at Warrington Bank Quay. (D.H.Mitchell)

Published 20 April 2013

ISBN 978 1 908174 40 6

© Middleton Press, 2013

Design Deborah Esher
Typesetting Barbara Mitchell

Published by
        Middleton Press
        Easebourne Lane
        Midhurst
        West Sussex
        GU29 9AZ
Tel: 01730 813169
Fax: 01730 812601
Email: info@middletonpress.co.uk
www.middletonpress.co.uk

Printed in the United Kingdom by Henry Ling Limited, at the Dorset Press, Dorchester, DT1 1HD

INDEX

ACKNOWLEDGEMENTS

We are very grateful for the assistance received from many of those mentioned in the credits also to B.W.L.Brooksbank, A.R.Carder, A.J.Castledine, G.Croughton, S.C.Jenkins, N.Langridge, J.P.McCrickard, Mr D. and Dr S.Salter, M.J.Stretton, T.Walsh and in particular, our always supportive wives, Barbara Mitchell and Janet Smith.

I. Railway Clearing House map for 1947.

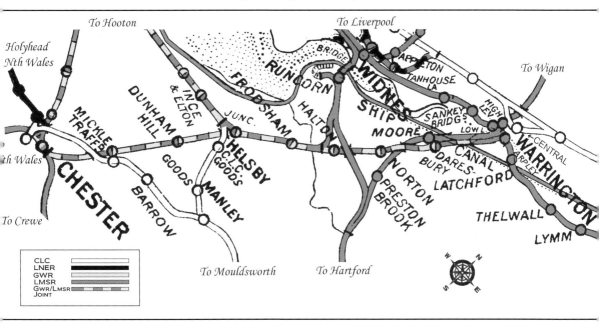

GEOGRAPHICAL SETTING

Of Roman origin, the important county town of Chester is situated on high ground in a U-shaped bend in the River Dee, which flows northwest to the sea. The line climbs through a cutting for one mile and then drops through others for a further mile, before reaching fairly level ground, south of the River Mersey.

The route crosses the River Gowy after another mile, this flowing north into the Mersey. The much larger River Weaver and the nearby Weaver Navigation are passed over between Frodsham and Runcorn.

Sutton Tunnel follows and the line descends, passing over the Keckwich Brook and the main line from Crewe. After almost two miles, it runs over the Manchester Ship Canal, plus the nearby River Mersey and enters Warrington on its final descent. This old market town was the first place upstream on the River Mersey to have a road bridge over it.

The route was built over various sandstones and within the county of Cheshire. The maps are to the scale of 25ins to 1 mile, with north at the top, unless otherwise indicated.

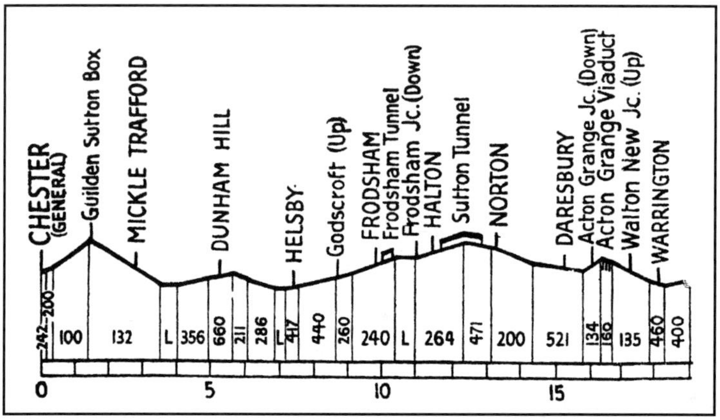

December 1895

Fares 1 cl.	Fares 2 cl.	Fares gov	Return 1 cl.	Return 2 cl.	Return gov		mrn	mrn	mrn	gov	gov	mrn	mrn	mrn	mrn	mrn	mrn	mrn	mrn	mrn	mrn	mrn	mrn
						Chester .... dep.	2 32	4 35	....	....	7 15	....	7 25	....	....	8 50	9 22	9 40	....	....	10 0	11 5	1145
0 6	0 4	0 3	0 10	0 7	0 6	Mickle Trafford....	Except Mondays. *Via* Warrington.	....	....	....	7 25	....	7 34	....	....	....	Mondays and Tuesdays.	9 47	....	....	....	1112	....
1 0	0 9	0 5	1 8	1 3	0 10	Dunham Hill		....	....	....	7 31	....	7 42	....	....	....		9 52	....	....	....	1117	....
1 4	1 0	0 7½	2 3	1 8	1 3	Helsby **312**........		....	....	....	'39	....	8g20	....	....	9 5		9 57	10 2	....	....	1122	1156
1 8	1 3	0 10	2 10	2 1	1 8	Frodsham		....	....	....	7 48	....	8 28	....	....	9 11		10 2	10 8	....	....	1127	12 2
2 6	1 9	1 2	4 3	3 0	2 4	**Runcorn 342**......		5 0	....	....	8 0	8 19	8 39	9 3	9 10	9 19		....	1015	....	1023	....	1213
2 10	2 2	1 6	4 11	3 10	2 11½	Ditton J. **344, 346**		**Mondays only.**	....	8 0	8 10	8 27	8 50	....	9 15	9 26		....	1021	....	1028	....	d
2 10	2 2	1 6	4 11	3 10	2 11½	Halebank..........			....	8 4	....	8 31	8 54	....	....	....		....	....	1024	....	....	....
2 10	2 2	1 6	4 11	3 10	2 11½	Speke..............			....	8 10	....	8 37	9 0	....	....	h		....	....	h	....	....	....
2 10	2 2	1 6	4 11	3 10	2 11½	Allerton **299**......			....	8 15	8 23	8 43	9 5	....	....	f		....	....	....	1037	....	1225
2 10	2 2	1 6	4 11	3 10	2 11½	Mossley Hill*......			....	8 20	....	8 48	9 10	....	....	....		....	....	1033	....	....	....
2 10	2 2	1 6	4 11	3 10	2 11½	Sefton Park......			....	8 23	....	8 51	....	....	....	....		....	....	....	....	....	....
2 10	2 2	1 6	4 11	3 10	2 11½	Wavertree....[272			8 10	8 25	....	8 53	....	....	....	....		....	....	....	....	....	....
2 10	2 2	1 6	4 11	3 10	2 11½	Edge Hill **355, 335,**	3 30	5 20	8 15	8 29	8 33	8 58	9 15	9 25	....	9 44	10 0	....	....	1038	1045	....	1235
2 10	2 2	1 6	4 11	3 10	2 11½	**Liverpool 310** arr.	3 35	5 25	8 20	8 35	8 40	9 5	9 20	9 30	....	9 50	10 5	....	....	1043	1050	....	1240

Continued below.

	aft	aft	aft	aft	aft	aft	aft	aft	aft	aft	aft	aft	aft	aft	aft	aft	aft	aft		SUNDAYS. *Via* Warrington. mrn	
Chester ......dep.	....	....	1 32	....	....	2 10	....	....	3 40	....	....	....	....	5 35	....	7 25	....	11 5	....	2 32	....
Mickle Trafford ...	....	....	....	....	....	2 17	....	....	....	....	....	....	....	5 42	....	7 32	....	....	....		....
Dunham Hill.....	....	....	....	....	....	2 22	....	....	....	....	....	....	....	5 50	....	i	....	....	....		....
Helsby **312**	....	1 15	....	....	....	2 27	2 40	....	....	....	....	....	....	....	6 16	7 41	....	Sig.	....		....
Frodsham	....	1 21	....	....	....	2 32	2 47	....	3 55	....	....	....	....	6 0	6 22	7 47	....	1122	....		....
Runcorn 342.....	1229	1 30	....	2 12	....	—	2 56	....	4 2	....	4 40	....	5 40	6 8	6 29	7 56	9 53	1131	....		....
Ditton J. **344, 346**	1235	1 37	....	2 17	2 24	....	3 0	3 51	....	....	4 46	5 30	5 45	....	6 36	8 2	9 59	Sat.	....		....
Halebank	1244	....	....	....	2 28	....	....	3 55	....	....	....	5 34	....	....	....	....	....	....	....		....
Speke.............	1250	....	....	....	2 33	....	....	4 0	....	....	....	5 40	....	....	....	....	....	....	....		....
Allerton **299**......	1255	....	....	....	2 37	....	....	4 6	f	....	....	5 45	f	6 21	....	....	....	j	....		....
Mossley Hill *	1 0	....	....	....	....	....	....	4 10	4 18	5 21	....	5 50	f	....	....	....	....	....	....		....
Sefton Park.......	1 5	....	....	....	....	....	....	4 12	....	....	....	5 54	....	....	....	....	....	....	....		....
Wavertree....[272	1 7	....	....	....	....	....	....	4 14	....	5 25	....	5 56	....	....	....	....	....	....	....		....
Edge Hill **355, 335,**	1 12	....	2 10	....	2 44	....	....	4 19	4 25	5 30	....	6 0	6 5	6 20	....	8 20	....	1150	....	3 30	....
Liverpool 310 arr.	1 17	....	2 15	....	2 50	....	....	4 25	4 30	5 35	....	6 5	6 10	6 35	....	8 25	....	1155	....	3 35	....

k Stops to set down on informing the Guard. l Stops to take up for Runcorn and beyond. * Station for Aigburth.

b Stops by signal to take up for Chester and beyond. c Stops to set down from Runcorn and beyond on informing Guard at Frodsham. d Stops to set down from beyond Chester on informing the Guard at Chester. e Arrives at 7 33 mrn. f Stop when required to set down. g Arrives at 7 49 mrn. h Stops to take up for Liverpool on informing Station Master. i Stops when required to take up for Runcorn and beyond. j Stops on Sats. when required to set down.

HISTORICAL BACKGROUND

The first line to reach Warrington was from the north and was opened by the Warrington & Newton Railway in 1831. Next was the Grand Junction Railway, which arrived from Crewe in 1837. The same company opened between Crewe and Chester in 1840. The Chester & Birkenhead Railway operated from the same year and the Shrewsbury & Chester Railway was running from 1846 from Wrexham.

Into this network came the Birkenhead, Lancashire & Cheshire Junction Railway, opening on 18th December 1850 and running between Chester and Warrington. It became known as the Birkenhead Joint Railway.

All these main lines remain open today. The opening dates of the later connections are given in the captions for the relevant junctions.

The subject of this album became the Birkenhead Railway in 1859. In 1860, it was under the joint management of the Great Western and London & North Western Railways. In 1923, this became the Great Western and London Midland & Scottish Joint Railway. Upon nationalisation in 1948 the route became part of the London Midland Region of British Railways. The northern two miles of the line however was never jointly managed, as the GJR had become part of the LNWR in 1846.

Privatisation brought North Western Trains running over the route from 2nd March 1997 on a seven year franchise and Arriva Trains Wales followed on 7th December 2003.

Electrification in the Warrington area took place on 23rd July 1973, it serving the Crewe-Preston route.

II. The 1946 edition is at 4 miles to 1 ins. The open circles represent closed stations.

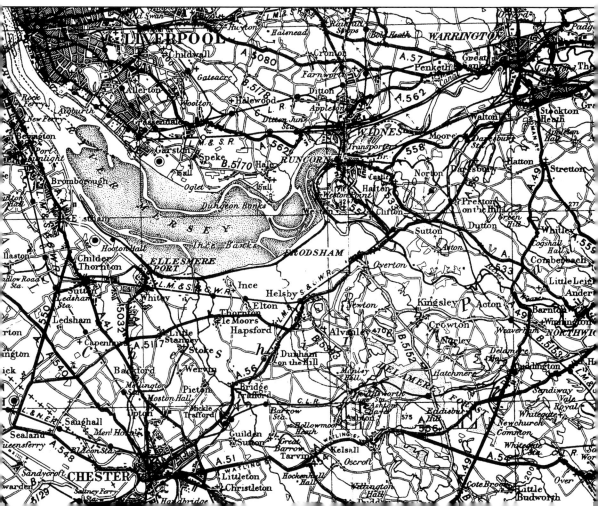

PASSENGER SERVICES

The table on the right gives an indication of the train frequency from Chester to Warrington, but excludes weekday services running on less than five days per week.

	Fast		Stopping	
	Weekdays	Sundays	Weekdays	Sundays
1865	3	0	3	2
1895	10	1	6	2
1925	14	1	7	2
1955	2	2	9	5
1985	5	8	10	0
2012	0	0	19	14

Additional trains ran between Chester and Frodsham, bound for Runcorn, most continuing to Liverpool (Lime Street), as opposite.

From 5th May 1975, the service was reduced to the 11.27 and 19.10 from Llandudno on Saturdays, in the Summer only. There was just one in the Winter. By September 2012, there was still only one train per week and it was in the Summer only. It was the 07.53 Chester to Runcorn and it met legal requirements.

	Fast		Stopping	
	Weekdays	Sundays	Weekdays	Sundays
1873	5	1	3	0
1895	4	0	7	0
1925	0	0	14	2
1955	0	1	9	3
1973	1	0	9	0

December 1895

MANCHESTER, WARRINGTON, FRODSHAM, and CHESTER.—Birkenhead.

CHESTER, FRODSHAM, WARRINGTON, ECCLES, and MANCHESTER.

Birkenhead—L. M. & S. and G. W.

Down. — Week Days.

Miles.	Down.	mrn	mrn H	mrn	mrn	mrn	mrn E	mrn S	mrn E	mrn	mrn	mrn	aft S	aft	aft	aft	aft	aft	aft E
	395 Llandudno ....dep.					6 20	7 52	7 35		8 45	8 45	9 45		1150			1 35		
	Chester (General).......dep.	2 20	4 25	7 12	7 55	8 24		9 5	9 10	1013	1035	1145	1222	1 42	2 20	2 25	3 35	4 12	4 35
2¾	Mickle Trafford			7 20							1042					2 31			4 41
5¼	Dunham Hill			7 29							1048					2 38			4 48
7¾	Helsby 404	Holyhead Express.		7 40	8 7	8 36		9 18	9 22	1025	1054	1158	1234	Holyhead Express.	2 32	2 44		4 27	4 55
9¾	Frodsham			7 50	8 12	8 41		9 24	9 28	1030	11 0	12 3	1239		2 38	2 50		4 32	5 2
11¼	Halton			7 58							11 5					2 56			5 7
13½	Norton			8 5							1110					3 1			5 12
15½	Daresbury			8 11		8 51					1115					3 6			5 17
18	Warrington A ... arr.	2 48	4 53	8 19	8 26	8 59	9 28	9 41	9 43	1043	1123	1218	1254	2 10	2 54	3 14	4 5	4 46	5 25
	316, 328, 432 ... dep.	2 53	5 1		8 28	9 2	9 31	9 46	9 48	1047		1223	1258	2 16	2 58		4 10	4 50	
23¼	Earlestown Junction 450				8 36												Bangor and Llandudno Express.	5 0	
24¾	Newton-le-Willows 328	3 8			8 39		Llandudno and Manchester Exp.			1058		1234						5 3	
27¼	Kenyon Junction 464				8 45							1241						5 9	
29½	Glazebury and Bury Lane																		
31¼	Astley																		
33¾	Barton Moss																		
35¼	Patricroft				8 56					1115									
36¾	Eccles 464, 466		Aa									Cc	1 22	Dd				5 24	
38¾	Cross Lane		Bb		Dd														
39	Ordsall Lane, for Salford																		
40	Manchester (Exchange). arr.	3 30	5 35		9 8	9 32	9 59	1018	1018	1130		1 d5	1 34	2 47	3 30		4 50	5 37	

Down. — Week Days—*Continued.*

Down.		aft	aft	aft		aft	aft	aft
395 Llandudno ....dep	Through Carriages, Portmadoc, Criccieth, and Pwllheli to Manchester, see page 398.	3 5		3a20	Through Carriages, Holyhead to Manchester daily, see page 398.	5 45	6 55	
Chester (General).......dep.		5 13	5 20	6 32		7 43	9 15	9 25
Mickle Trafford			5 27	6 38				9 32
Dunham Hill			5 33	6 45				9 38
Helsby 404		5 25	5 41	6 53			9 27	9 44
Frodsham			5 48	7 0			9 32	9 49
Halton			5 53	7 5				9 54
Norton			5 57	7 10				9 59
Daresbury			6 2	7 15				10 4
Warrington A ... arr.		5 43	6 17	7 21		8 11	9 48	1010
316, 328, 432 ... dep.		5 46		7 25		8 16	9 51	
Earlestown Junction 450		5 55		7 33			10 1	
Newton-le-Willows 328		5 58		7 36			10 7	
Kenyon Junction 464						8 30		
Glazebury and Bury Lane								
Astley								
Barton Moss								
Patricroft				7 52		8 43	1022	
Eccles 464, 466		6 13		7 58		8 47	1026	
Cross Lane						Kk		
Ordsall Lane, for Salford								
Manchester (Exchange). arr.		6 26		8 10		9 0	1040	

Down. — Sundays.

Down.	mrn	aft	aft
399 Llandudno ....dep.		1 20	4 25
Chester (General).......dep.	7 0	3 10	7 15
Mickle Trafford	7 7		
Dunham Hill	7 15		7 25
Helsby 404	7 25		7 35
Frodsham	7 40		7 40
Halton	7 46		7 48
Norton	7 53		
Daresbury	8 0		7 59
Warrington A ... arr.	8 10	3 38	8 7
324, 332, 432 ... dep.	8 20	3 41	8 12
Earlestown Junction 451	8 30		8 22
Newton-le-Willows 332	8h50	3 51	8 26
Kenyon Junction 464			8 34
Glazebury and Bury Lane			
Astley			
Barton Moss			
Patricroft	9n20		8 47
Eccles 464, 466	9 23	4 10	8 52
Cross Lane			
Ordsall Lane, for Salford			
Manchester (Exchange). arr.	9 43	4 25	9 5

n Arrives at 9 4 mrn.

S or *s* Saturdays only.

NOTES.

- **A** Bank Quay; about ¾ mile to Central Station.
- **Aa** Stops at Eccles to set down from Ireland on notice being given to the Guard.
- *a* Departs Llandudno at 4 30 aft, on Saturdays.
- **Bb** Stops at Cross Lane on Fridays to set down from Ireland on notice being given to the Guard.
- **Cc** Stops on Saturdays to set down.
- **Dd** Stops to set down on informing the Guard.
- *d* Arrives at 1 13 aft. on Saturdays.
- **E** or *e* Except Saturdays.
- **H** Except Mondays.
- *h* Arrives at 8 34 mrn.
- **Kk** Stops on Mondays to set down from beyond Chester on informing the Guard.

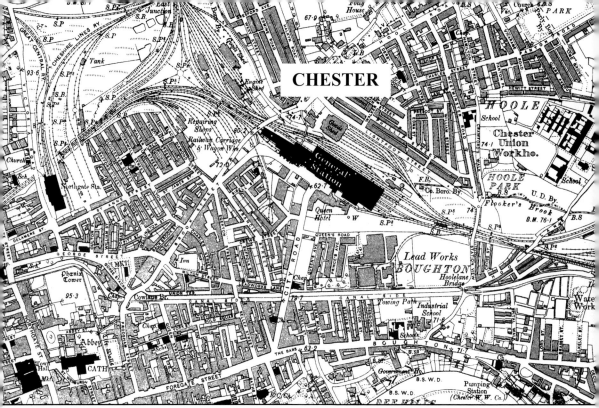

CHESTER

III.   The 1913 edition at 6ins to 1 mile has the route from Crewe of the LNWR on the right. It is the lower one and above it is the joint line to Warrington, which we will follow. The triangle top left has the Birkenhead route at the top and lines to North Wales and Shrewsbury on the left. They pass under the lines serving the Northgate terminus, which was in use from 1875 until 6th October 1969. The main station was completed in 1848 and was usually known as Chester General until 1970. It was a joint venture from the outset, with three companies being involved initially. The black area represents the extent of the massive roof; compare it with the cathedral, lower left. The Shropshire Union Canal runs across this extract. The first LNWR engine shed was within the triangle, but from 1870 it was close to the start of the line to Crewe. The GWR engine shed is shown east of the southern apex of the triangle.

1.   We start our survey with three views at the west end of the station. On the left is the bridge at the north end of Brook Street and resting between duties is no. 79, a GWR Armstrong outside framed "Standard Goods". (G.Coltas Trust/Bentley coll.)

2.   Turning a few degrees to the right on 11th July 1941, the long footbridge comes into view, together with the inclined ramp which provided road access to the LMS goods yard. Centre is 0-4-2T no. 3579, of class 3571. (H.C.Casserley)

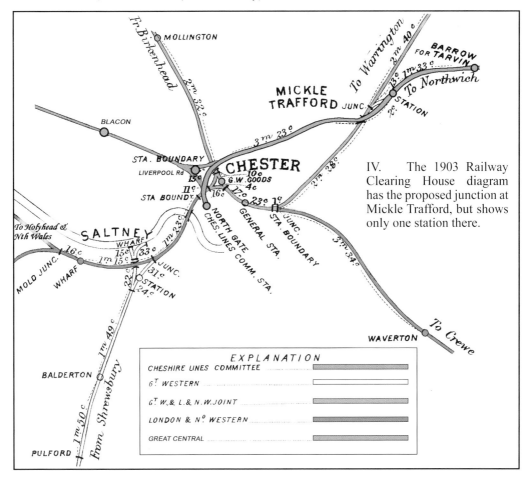

IV.   The 1903 Railway Clearing House diagram has the proposed junction at Mickle Trafford, but shows only one station there.

3.　　It is 24th April 1947 and this panorama is from the long footbridge and includes the road down to the goods yard. The nearest wagon was the battered property of the Cooperative Wholesale Society. (H.C.Casserley)

L. & N. W. & G. W. Joint Rys
Issued subject to the conditions & regulations in the Cos Time Tables Books Bills & Notices.

MICKLE TRAFFORD　TO
FRODSHAM
Third]　995(S)　[Class
FRODSHAM　FARE -/7

NO 1 7　2421

L.M.S.&G.W.J'tRys
FOR CONDITIONS SEE NOTICES

DUNHAM HILL　TO
HELSBY
THIRD
CLASS]　447(S)　FARE-/5 P
HELSBY

3747　3747

4.   An indifferent record from 1948 is from the middle of the down through platform, near the booking hall. The structures between the rails were to prevent staff tripping on point rods. Note that there were two through lines at that time. Most glass had been lost during the bombing of World War II. (Stations UK)

5.   Both footbridges are evident as ex-LMS 4-6-0 class 5 no. 45238 passes through with an up parcels train on 22nd August 1966. Most of the extensive roof had been dismantled in the 1950s. (T.Heavyside)

6.   This array of ex-LNWR signals faced drivers of up trains in June 1974. In the left background is No. 2 Box. (R.S.Carpenter coll.)

7.   The splendid 1848 structure was little changed when photographed on 31st October 1981. The clock is deliberately off centre (behind the lamp post), so that it can be seen by those arriving along City Road. There are two carved wooden owls, which are deemed to deter feral pigeons from roosting. (D.A.Thompson)

L. & N. W. & G. W. Joint Rys.
Issued subject to the conditions & regulations in the Cos Time Tables Books Bills & Notices.
DUNHAM HILL TO
WARRINGTON
Third] 447(S) [Class
WARRINGTON FARE 1·1
5791

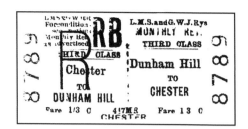

L.M.S. and G.W.J. Rys.
MONTHLY RET.
THIRD CLASS
Dunham Hill
TO
CHESTER
Fare 1·3 C
8789

THIRD CLASS
Chester
TO
DUNHAM HILL
Fare 1/3 C 447MR
CHESTER

8. The main building is in the background as DMU no. T592 waits at platform 2 to work to Helsby on 27th June 1988. It will run north up the Birkenhead line to Hooton, where it will reverse to proceed via Ellesmere Port. (S.Rickard/J&J coll.)

9.   The main building is on the left in this view from 5th May 2000. EWS no. 66191 is coming off the goods lines, while working from Dee Marsh Junction to Warrington Arpley. The location is East Junction New and the trussed roofs behind the train are over bay platforms nos 5 and 6, also the through platforms, 4 and 7. (P.D.Shannon)

→ 10. Entering platform 4 on 12th May 2011 at 11.49 are class 5MT 4-6-0s nos 44871 *Sovereign* and 45407 *The Lancashire Fusilier*. They were heading "The Cathedrals Explorer", an 8-day tour of Britain with steam haulage on most of it. (V.Mitchell)

Other views can be found in our
Chester to Birkenhead,
Chester to Rhyl,
***Stafford to Chester* and**
***Shrewsbury to Chester* albums.**
Also *Chester Tramways* for more
local transport history.

→ 11. Minutes later and we can see that platform 4 is divided into two parts. It can accommodate 15 coaches, as can No. 7, while No. 3 takes 18. Beyond the brick arches is the through line; it is signalled for reversible running, as are the two adjacent platform lines. (V.Mitchell)

12.   A view from the other end of the footbridge on 17th November 2012 has the main entrance on the left with the ticket machines centre. All the glass was clean and the truss sheeting, seen in picture 8, had gone. (H.Ballantyne)

13.   Only one platform had a conductor rail and this was No. 7. It came into use on 7th October 1993 and was used by trains to Liverpool via Hooton. Seen on 17th November 2012 is no. 150110 after arrival from Warrington. These platforms were opened in 1890 and all were renumbered on 5th October 1980. (H.Ballantyne)

14.   The Crewe lines are on the right and the Warrington route passes under the bridge in this eastward view from November 1964. No. 1 Box is beyond the signal gantry, which is of LNWR origin. Lower left is part of the bridge carrying Station View; we cross to the other side of it for our next vista. (R.J.Essery/R.S.Carpenter coll.)

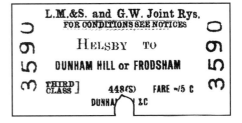

15.   The station is in the distance and part of No. 2 Box is on the left, close to the Crewe lines.
The short semaphore arms were for shunting movements on the Warrington route.
(R.J.Essery/R.S.Carpenter coll.)

16.   A Leicester to Llandudno service is seen arriving from Warrington on 7th July 1973, hauled by Peak class 45 no. 98 *Royal Engineer*. The 1958 No. 1 Box had only two months of action left. (T.Heavyside)

17.   We swap bridges that day to witness a DMU arriving from Crewe, while class 40 no. 207 takes empty stock from North Wales onto the Warrington line. No. 2 Box is beyond the brick bridge. (T.Heavyside)

18.	A short walk on 13th August 1982 takes us closer to No. 2 Box, which almost totally obscures the station. Bypassing it is no. 47192 with coal bound for Fiddlers Ferry. The former LNWR goods shed is on the right. This box lasted until 4th May 1984, when Crewe Power Signal Box took over. It was built beyond the right border of the picture. (P.D.Shannon)

SOUTH OF MICKLE TRAFFORD

19.	Showing its Crosti boiler, class 9F 2-10-0 no. 92021 runs towards Chester on 20th August 1966. It has passed under the skew bridge, which was opened by the Cheshire Lines Committee in 1874. It will soon pass Guilden Sutton signal box, which lasted until 13th April 1969. (H.Ballantyne)

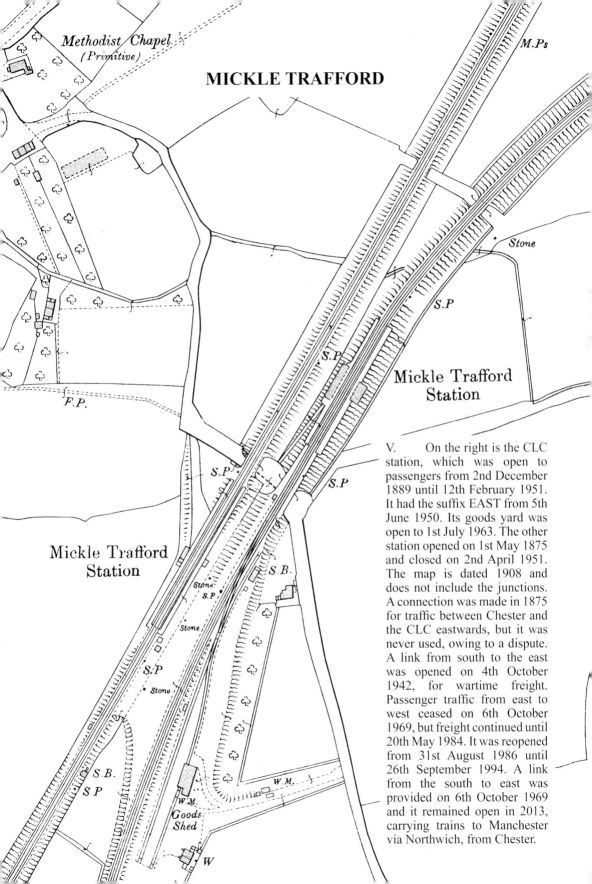

Methodist Chapel
(Primitive)

MICKLE TRAFFORD

M.Ps

Stone

S.P

S.P

Mickle Trafford
Station

F.P.

S.P

S.P

Mickle Trafford
Station

S.B.

Stone
S.P.

Stone

S.P

Stone

S.P

W.M.

S.B.

S P

W.M.

Goods
Shed

W

V.   On the right is the CLC station, which was open to passengers from 2nd December 1889 until 12th February 1951. It had the suffix EAST from 5th June 1950. Its goods yard was open to 1st July 1963. The other station opened on 1st May 1875 and closed on 2nd April 1951. The map is dated 1908 and does not include the junctions. A connection was made in 1875 for traffic between Chester and the CLC eastwards, but it was never used, owing to a dispute. A link from south to the east was opened on 4th October 1942, for wartime freight. Passenger traffic from east to west ceased on 6th October 1969, but freight continued until 20th May 1984. It was reopened from 31st August 1986 until 26th September 1994. A link from the south to east was provided on 6th October 1969 and it remained open in 2013, carrying trains to Manchester via Northwich, from Chester.

20.   Our first three views are from 1949. Here we look southwest, between the stations, the former CLC one being on the left. We move along the platform on the right for the next viewpoint. (Stations UK)

21.   The connection of 1942 comes into view, as does the former LNWR signal box. This was closed on 7th September 1969. It was not a location to choose on a stormy day. The edge of the village is top left on the map; its population rose from 268 in 1901 to 348 in 1961. (Stations UK)

22.   Moving further south along the same platform, we gain a panorama, which includes both stations. Both had foot access from the west side only, with a foot crossing over the tracks to the eastern platforms. The GWR recorded a revenue of £10 here for 1913 and 1923, but only £1 for 1932. (Stations UK)

23.   The junction was recorded in about 1960, with a down train and much unused track bed. The 2-6-0 is an ex-Lancashire & Yorkshire Railway "Crab" and is running to Chester General, the nearer tracks being those to Chester Northgate, ex-CLC. The LNWR platforms had been on the left. The connection in the foreground lasted until 1992. (Bentley coll.)

24.	This signal box opened on 7th September 1969 for freight traffic between the south and east, passenger services on that route starting four weeks later. Its 35-lever frame was still in use in 2013. (Milepost 92½)

VI.	The 1927 revision at 2 miles to 1ins has our route diagonally and the CLC line with curves. There was no connection between the two at that time. The diagram is from 1990 and shows the position of the signal box.

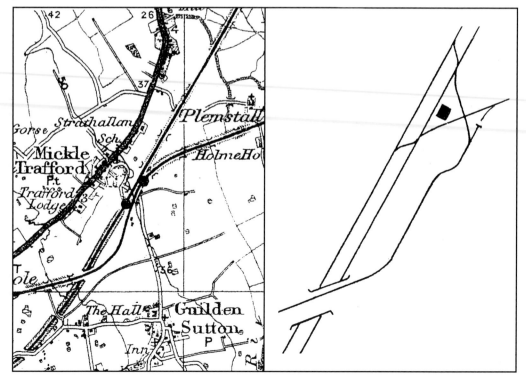

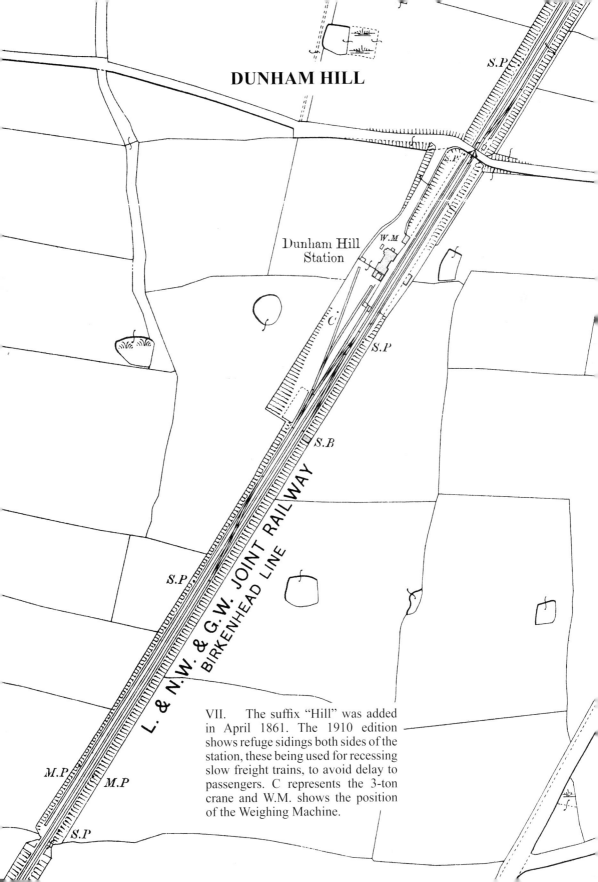

DUNHAM HILL

S.P.

Dunham Hill
Station

W.M

S.P.

C

S.P.

S.B

L. & N.W. & G.W. JOINT RAILWAY

BIRKENHEAD LINE

S.P.

M.P

M.P

S.P.

VII.   The suffix "Hill" was added
in April 1861. The 1910 edition
shows refuge sidings both sides of the
station, these being used for recessing
slow freight trains, to avoid delay to
passengers. C represents the 3-ton
crane and W.M. shows the position
of the Weighing Machine.

25.   A southward view from the road bridge in 1949 includes the parcels shed on the right and the flat roofed signal box in the distance. This was one of two opened on 19th July 1942 to control access to the new War Department Depot. There were 28 buildings. No. 1 Box closed on 2nd September 1969; No. 2 had closed on 25th November 1951, but stood derelict for 57 years. The GWR income here was £79 in 1903 and £47 in 1933. (Stations UK)

26.   Turning round, we see the simple facilities, which were in use until 7th April 1952. The goods yard closed on 7th May 1956. The Royal Ordnance Factory had two new Fowler diesel engines when it opened, but they left before the site closed in 1964. It had been an emergency food store in its later years. (Stations UK)

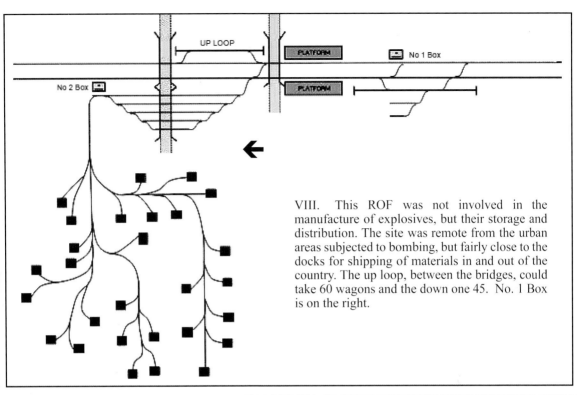

VIII. This ROF was not involved in the manufacture of explosives, but their storage and distribution. The site was remote from the urban areas subjected to bombing, but fairly close to the docks for shipping of materials in and out of the country. The up loop, between the bridges, could take 60 wagons and the down one 45. No. 1 Box is on the right.

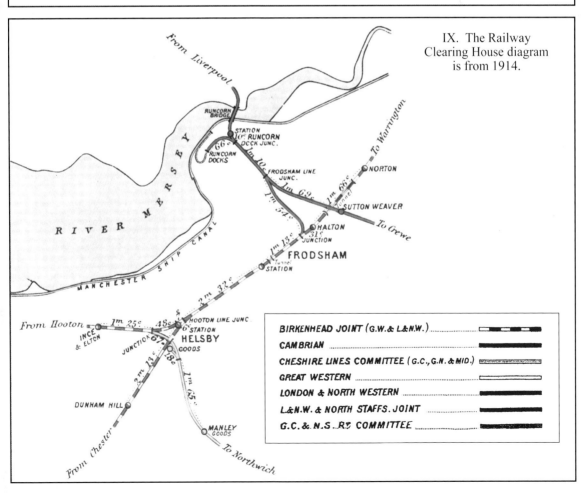

IX. The Railway Clearing House diagram is from 1914.

BIRKENHEAD JOINT (G.W. & L.&N.W.)	
CAMBRIAN	
CHESHIRE LINES COMMITTEE (G.C., G.N. & MID.)	
GREAT WESTERN	
LONDON & NORTH WESTERN	
L.&N.W. & NORTH STAFFS. JOINT	
G.C. & N.S. R? COMMITTEE	

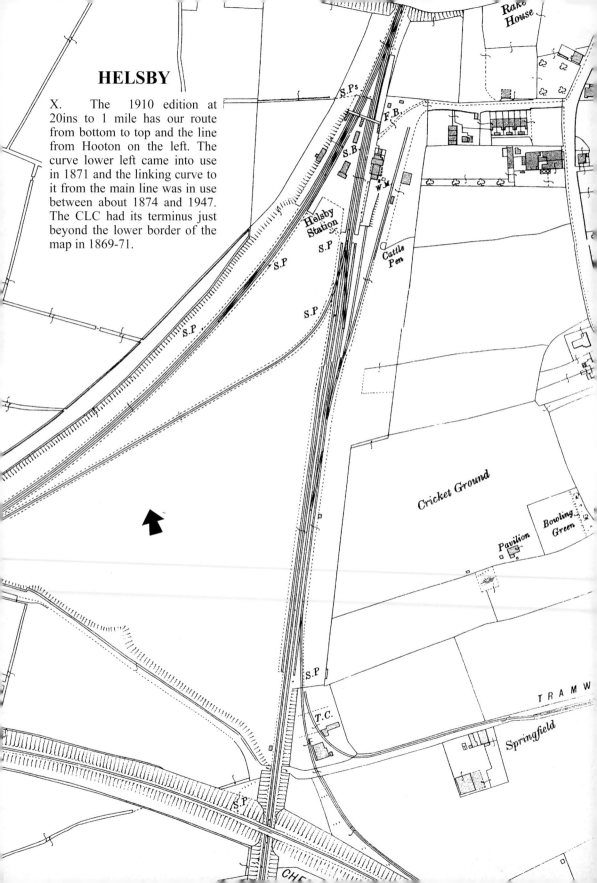

HELSBY

X. The 1910 edition at 20ins to 1 mile has our route from bottom to top and the line from Hooton on the left. The curve lower left came into use in 1871 and the linking curve to it from the main line was in use between about 1874 and 1947. The CLC had its terminus just beyond the lower border of the map in 1869-71.

27.   A train from Chester is centre, while the line from Hooton is on the right. The station yard shines brightly, as it had probably just been surfaced for the first time. The GWR had 421 tickets issued in 1903 and 132 in 1933. (P.Laming coll.)

28.   A train departs for Warrington, while a connecting service from the Ellesmere Port line waits on the right. Roofing had been added to the footbridge at this busy junction.
(Lens of Sutton coll.)

29.   This northward view is probably from the early 1930s. Two of the three covered stairways are included, as is the signal box, which was still in use about 80 years later. (R.S.Carpenter coll.)

30.   The same road bridge is seen again, but the train is running over the points to the Hooton line. The 2-8-0 is hauling tankers destined for the massive Stanlow Oil Refinery, only about five miles along the line. (Bentley coll.)

31.   The loading gauge is visible on the left and an exchange siding curves to the right behind the notice board. BR class 5 no. 73134 is arriving from Chester on 10th October 1959. (H.C.Casserley)

32.   The signal box was built in 1900 and had 45 levers. It is 26th November 1964 and students of sanitary engineering can appreciate the outstanding structure. The long brush avoided the need for a lengthy ladder. (R.J.Essery/R.S.Carpenter)

33.   The low height of the platform is evident in this record of the waiting room on the same day. Gas lighting prevails. (R.J.Essery/R.S.Carpenter)

Other views can be seen in pictures 112 to 120 in our
Chester to Birkenhead **album.**

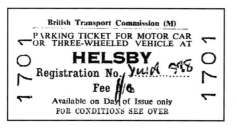

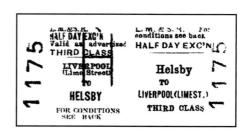

34. The goods yard had been to the left of the train until it was closed on 3rd February 1964. It had a 5-ton crane and a small cattle pen. No. 5036 hauls freight from Chester on 22nd August 1973 and runs alongside the refuge siding. In the background is the former CLC line linking Stanlow and Mouldsworth. (T.Heavyside)

35. Seen on the same day, the footbridge had lost its roof, but the buildings had retained their fine detailing. Arriving is the 16.30 Manchester to Llandudno DMU. (T.Heavyside)

36.   A goods siding had once extended as far as the lorry. Seen on 1st June 1984 is no. 45124 with the 11.15 Bangor to Newcastle service. (H.Ballantyne)

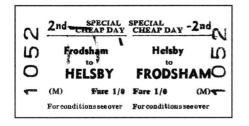

1052   2nd SPECIAL   SPECIAL 2nd   2501
CHEAP DAY   CHEAP DAY
Frodsham   Helsby
to   to
HELSBY   FRODSHAM
(M)   Fare 1/0   Fare 1/0   (M)
For conditions see over   For conditions see over

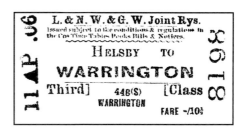

11AP.06   L. & N. W. & G. W. Joint Rys.   8198
Issued subject to the conditions & regulations in
the Cos Time Tables Books Bills & Notices.
HELSBY   TO
WARRINGTON
Third]   448(S)   [Class
WARRINGTON
FARE -/10½

37.	A panorama from the footbridge on 27th February 1987 features the 13.22 from Crewe to Manchester Victoria. The former exchange siding was in use by the engineers. (T.Heavyside)

38.	No. 150226 was working the 18.22 Chester to Hull on 6th August 1987, by which time stylish housing had replaced the neglected yard. It is leaving platform 2, which takes four cars, while No. 1 (left) takes seven. (T.Heavyside)

39.　The CLC bridge was still visible on 27th March 2002 as no. 158754 arrived from Chester. Local supporters had provided the daffodils and station enhancement. The bridge had been in use between 1871 and 1991. It now carries a path. (P.D.Shannon)

40.　Working the 07.15 Ellesmere Port to Crewe on 25th July 2011 was no. 70006, in pristine condition. Since 1993, there had been only a token passenger service, on weekdays only, from here to Ellesmere Port. (P.D.Shannon)

NATIONAL RAILWAY HERITAGE AWARDS

THE WESTINGHOUSE SIGNALLING AWARD
PRESENTED TO
NETWORK RAIL
FOR
HELSBY SIGNAL BOX
BY
HRH
THE DUKE OF GLOUCESTER
KG GCVO
2004

41.   The retention of the original stone buildings, plus the historic signal box, makes this an unusual location on the national network. (A.C.Hartless)

42.   No. 175003 is working the 09.45 Llandudno to Manchester Piccadilly on 17th November 2012. The mixture of ancient and modern details makes this a fascinating place to visit. (H.Ballantyne)

SOUTH OF FRODSHAM

43.   About halfway between Helsby and Frodsham was Godscraft Box, on the up side. It broke the section and was usually open only in the Summer, when the route was particularly busy. The stove is alight as BR class 5 no. 73093 approaches. (Bentley coll.)

44.   Another undated view and this includes class 8F no. 48448, but we have no other details. The box closed on 13th September 1965. The signal arms were removed during the closure periods. (Bentley coll.)

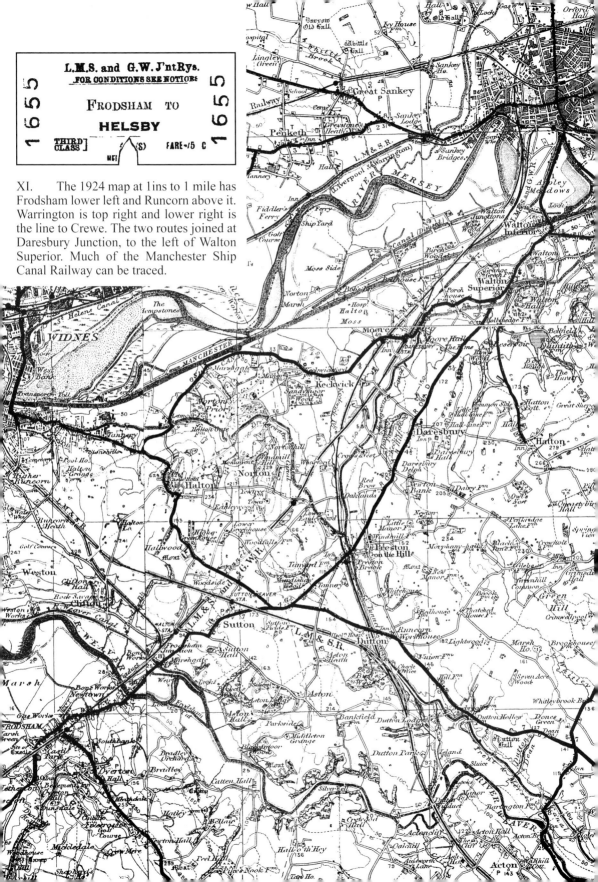

L.M.S. and G.W. J'nt Rys.
FOR CONDITIONS SEE NOTICES

FRODSHAM TO
HELSBY

1655

THIRD
CLASS ⌐ (S)   FARE -/5 C

XI.　　The 1924 map at 1ins to 1 mile has Frodsham lower left and Runcorn above it. Warrington is top right and lower right is the line to Crewe. The two routes joined at Daresbury Junction, to the left of Walton Superior. Much of the Manchester Ship Canal Railway can be traced.

FRODSHAM

XII. The 1911 survey indicates the good proximity of the station to the town centre and to the jam works, no doubt a good customer of the railways. The 1938 handbook lists a crane rated at 3 tons.

45.   Vans are visible in the western part of the goods yard as a train arrives from Warrington. A lengthy seat was provided, the local population being 4131 in 1901. There were 421 GWR tickets issued here in 1923, but only 191 by 1935. (Lens of Sutton coll.)

46.   This card was postmarked 15-11-1905 and shows the obligatory staff presentation, plus a personal weighing machine. These usually required a payment of 1d in the slot. (P.Laming coll.)

47.   On the right is the goods shed; freight continued until 3rd February 1964. The number of residents rose to 5661 by 1961. Even the flower beds had received colouring on this postcard. (P.Laming coll.)

48.   Lamp cleaning is an unusual subject for a photograph, probably from the 1930s. The Suggs lanterns were still in production in the 21st century, using 19th century tooling. (Stations UK)

49.   Access to both goods yards can be seen in this undated record of a southbound train. The sandstone is at the northern limit of the outcrop, which carries Delamere Forest. The locomotive is BR class 4 4-6-0 no. 75010. (Bentley coll.)

50.　　The signal box was of LNWR origin and had a 25-lever frame. Class 5 4-6-0 no. 45204 is working a local train on 2nd August 1958, composed entirely of compartment stock. The tunnel and the Methodist Church are in the view. (R.S.Carpenter)

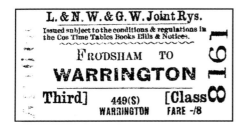

51.　　The box is in the distance and closed on 26th July 1968. The goods office and its solitary chimney are evident in this panorama from 10th October 1959. The jam factory chimney is on the right. (H.C.Casserley)

52.　　A southward panorama from the footbridge on 9th August 1975 features no. 25283 leading no. 25058, with tankers from Stanlow Refinery. The station became partially unstaffed in the following year. (T.Heavyside)

53.　　No. 45026 was working the 11.15 Bangor to Newcastle on 17th August 1984. Sadly one platform had lost its traditional waiting room, but this footbridge retained its non-original boarding. (D.H.Mitchell)

54.　　Recorded on the same day was M51184 working the 10.41 Manchester Victoria to Llandudno service. The public footpath retained its railings within the lattice bridge structure. (D.H.Mitchell)

55.   Part of Stanlow Refinery is visible in the distance, as no. 37714 runs through on 28th August 1989, bound for Warrington Yard. The former loading dock can be seen on the right. (T.Heavyside)

56.   An improved shelter had arrived by the time Pacer no. 142060 was recorded running in on 23rd July 2001. It was working the 14.17 Manchester Victoria to Llandudno. A second shelter is on the left. (A.C.Hartless)

57.   Running between the same stations on 17th November 2012 is no. 175107. The historic building had just received a major renovation, but the platform had lost its ancient paving. (H.Ballantyne)

NORTH OF FRODSHAM
Frodsham Tunnel

58. The tunnel is only 87 yards in length and carries the A56, so numbered in 1919. Photographed in 1958 is the north portal. (R.S.Carpenter)

59. The tunnel is in the distance as no. 142054 runs close to the trackbed of the headshunt of the goods yard. It is working the 12.20 Stalybridge to Bangor service on 28th August 1989 and giving some passengers a close view of the deformed sedimentary strata. (T.Heavyside)

Weaver Viaduct

60. Another Manchester to Llandudno train is seen, this time behind no. 40080 on 25th August 1979. In the distance is the viaduct carrying the M56 over the Weaver Valley. The trio of elderly barges adds to the diversity of transport eras represented. (T.Heavyside)

61. The viaduct is seen from the other side on 20th May 1980, as no. 25294 hauls 4-6-2 no. 4498 *Sir Nigel Gresley* and "Black Five" 4-6-0 no. 5000 to the Rocket 150 event. The A56 bridge is in the background. (T.Heavyside)

62. Featured is the River Weaver, plus its viaduct, on 4th September 2010. No. 46115 *Scots Guardsman* is a 4-6-0 of the LMS "Royal Scot" class and is hauling the "Lune River Trust" special. (H.Ballantyne)

Weston Viaduct

63. Unlike its near neighbour, only one long span was required in this viaduct. No. 40144 is bound for Chester on 27th July 1974. The location is lower left on the next map. (T.Heavyside)

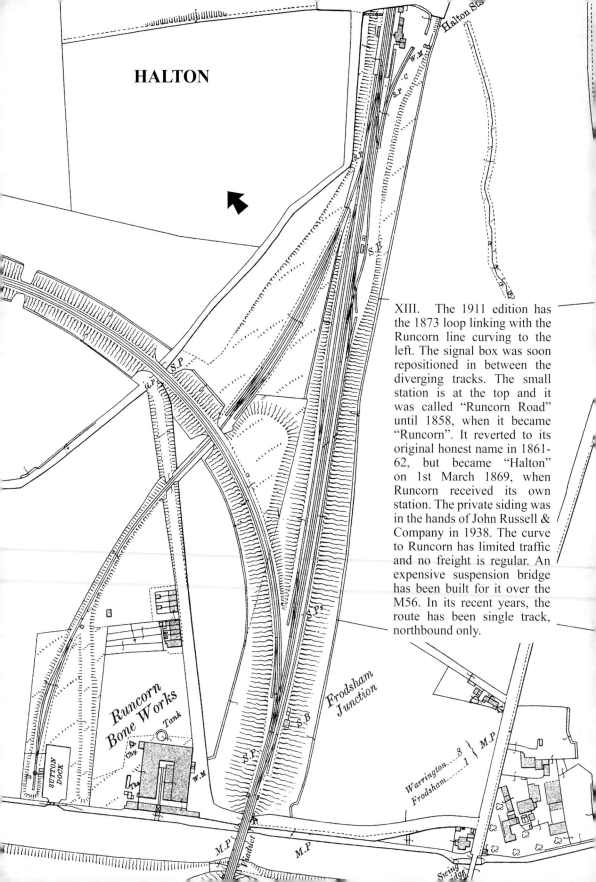

HALTON

XIII. The 1911 edition has the 1873 loop linking with the Runcorn line curving to the left. The signal box was soon repositioned in between the diverging tracks. The small station is at the top and it was called "Runcorn Road" until 1858, when it became "Runcorn". It reverted to its original honest name in 1861-62, but became "Halton" on 1st March 1869, when Runcorn received its own station. The private siding was in the hands of John Russell & Company in 1938. The curve to Runcorn has limited traffic and no freight is regular. An expensive suspension bridge has been built for it over the M56. In its recent years, the route has been single track, northbound only.

Runcorn Bone Works

Frodsham Junction

SUTTON DOCK

Warrington...8
Frodsham...1

64.	This view north has Sutton Tunnel in the distance and shows the platform extensions and ramp, which do not appear on the map. The summit is in the tunnel and so the water column would have been welcomed by many drivers. GWR tickets issued numbered 98 in 1913 and 9 in 1933. (R.S.Carpenter coll.)

65.	A 1949 record in the same direction includes the hose (known as the bag) and the other platform access, although the steps are not in the same direction as those on the map. Three 1949 pictures follow. (Stations UK)

66.   The signal box had 40 levers and lasted until 2nd July 1967. The goods yard closed on 3rd February 1964, its crane being rated at five tons. (Stations UK)

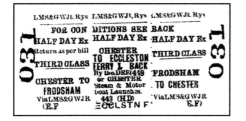

67.   An up express approaches, while we gain a glimpse of the loading dock in the goods yard. The unusual arrangement of the signals was due to their view being impeded by the low bridge, shown below. (Stations UK)

68.   The extended platforms and the tunnel come into sight again. Close to the bridge are the obligatory fire buckets and the parcels shed. (Stations UK)

69.   The 11.22 Chester to Manchester Victoria on 12th August 1983 has run by Frodsham Junction Box. This was opened with 32 levers by the LNWR in 1912 and was still in use in 2013. The Runcorn link is hidden by the hill on the right. The line on the left was known as the Up Goods Loop. (D.H.Mitchell)

70.   No. 387 has just run through Sutton Tunnel on 7th June 1973 with the 11.30 Manchester to Llandudno. Part of the train is under the M56 bridge. The main line between Crewe and Liverpool passes over the tunnel. (T.Heavyside)

71.   This and the previous picture were taken from the bridge seen in picture 68. No. 150134 is working the 14.49 Liverpool Lime Street to Ellesmere Port via Rainhill on 27th March 2002. It was the only such regular journey each weekday at that time. (P.D.Shannon)

72.   Moving closer to the south portal, we can enjoy its castellations as a Claughton class 4-6-0 emerges with an express. The lower signal arm was probably an all-red ancient distant signal from the days prior to their standardisation in yellow. A chevron is just visible.
(R.S.Carpenter coll.)

73. We are at the north portal in bad weather as a group rest is taken. The tunnel length is 1 mile 154yds. (Bentley coll.)

74. Once a common treat, the view from the front seat of an original BR DMU could be enjoyed at no extra cost. This shot at the north end is from July 1974. (M.Dart)

NORTON (CHESHIRE)

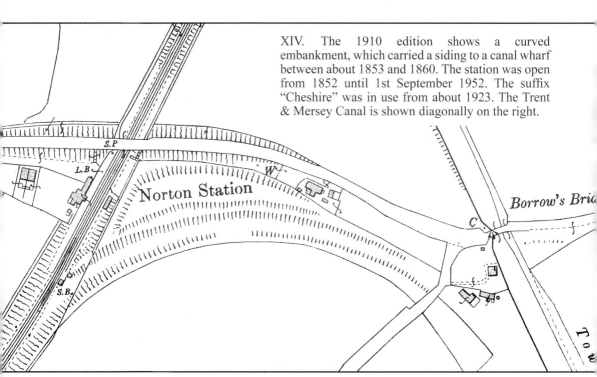

XIV. The 1910 edition shows a curved embankment, which carried a siding to a canal wharf between about 1853 and 1860. The station was open from 1852 until 1st September 1952. The suffix "Cheshire" was in use from about 1923. The Trent & Mersey Canal is shown diagonally on the right.

75. No. 45441 was a class 5 4-6-0 of a type introduced by the LMS in 1934. Access to the nearest platform was by steps from the road. They are behind the telegraph pole. The GWR sold 68 tickets in 1913 and 4 in 1931. (Bentley coll.)

76.   No. 73044 was also class 5, but of a type built by BR from 1951 onwards, at Doncaster. Part of Norton signal box is on the right. It was built by the LNWR and was in use until 3rd September 1972. (Bentley coll.)

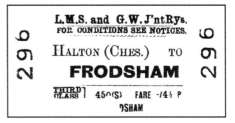

RUNCORN EAST

77.   The station was built 300yds to the south of Norton's and it opened on 3rd October 1983. It is seen on 19th May 2012, with no. 175112 running from Llandudno to Manchester Piccadilly. The platforms were designed for nine coaches. (T.Heavyside)

→   78. No. 175104 is working the same service in the opposite direction on 17th November 2012. In the background is Norton's replacement signal box, which had ten levers and controlled the crossover in front of it. Fresh housing associated with Runcorn New Town justified the station, which was supported by Warrington Development Corporation. (H.Ballantyne)

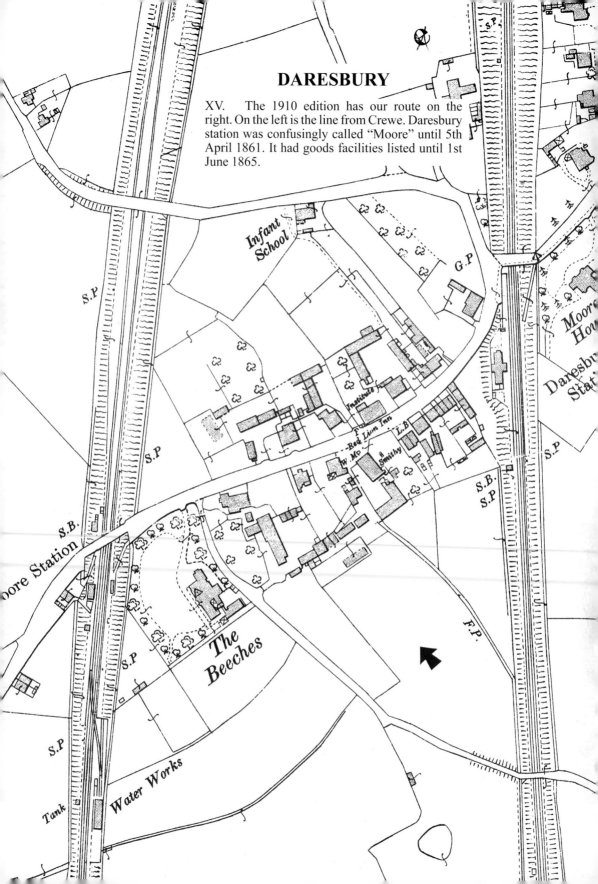

DARESBURY

XV. The 1910 edition has our route on the right. On the left is the line from Crewe. Daresbury station was confusingly called "Moore" until 5th April 1861. It had goods facilities listed until 1st June 1865.

Infant School

Institute

Red Lion Inn

Smithy

L.B

W. Mo

G.P

S.P

S.P

S.P

S.P

S.P

S.P

S.P

S.B.

S.B.

S.B.
S.P

Moore Hou

Daresbu
Stat

oore Station

The Beeches

F.P.

Tank

Water Works

79.	Looking southeast in 1947, a poor camera allows an impression of the signal box, which was in use until 9th December 1956. It was then replaced by a flat-roofed box with 25 levers. This lasted until 3rd September 1972. (Stations UK)

80.	A better view in the other direction in 1959 includes two impressive waste vent pipes, plus ornate chimney pots. The population was 153 in 1901, this rising to 283 by 1961. However, the station was closed on 7th July 1952. It had sold 15 GWR tickets in 1903 and 30 in 1933. (Stations UK)

NORTH OF DARESBURY

81.   Daresbury Box is seen in 1967. Its 25-lever frame was in use from 9th December 1956 until 3rd September 1972. We are looking south and on the left are two sidings, which formed the Chester lines until the mid-1890s, when they had to be moved and raised onto a bridge over the Manchester Ship Canal, then under construction. The Crewe lines also had to be raised. (Stations UK)

XVI.   The deviation in the Chester route is evident, lower left. Its continuation north of the canal to Old Main Line Junction is also shown. This was the northern limit of the Joint Line. The RCH diagram is from 1901. The Crewe route was not subject to any deviation, only elevation.

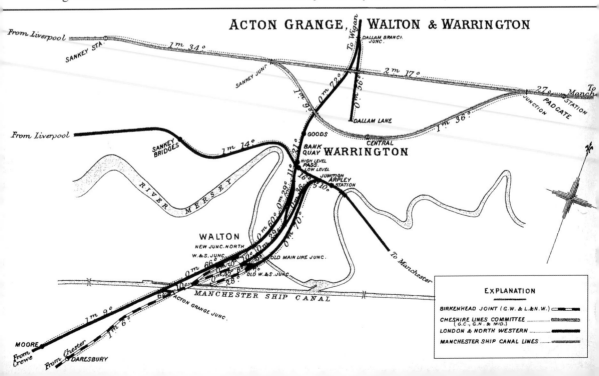

SOUTH OF WARRINGTON
Acton Grange Junction

82. The 12.57 Scarborough to Bangor has just run over the junction on 8th August 1983, hauled by no. 45070. Evident is the overhead electrification of the Crewe to Warrington line, which came into use on 7th January 1973. (D.H.Mitchell)

83. The junction signals can be seen again, but the wiring is less clear due to the weather and tree growth. No. 47195 is working chemicals the short distance from Arpley to Ellesmere Port on 8th July 1991. (P.D.Shannon)

84. No. 87030 is working an express to London on 17th October 1987 and is passing over the connections between the two routes. The Chester lines are in the foreground and their wires terminate behind the camera. (P.D.Shannon)

➜ XVII. As stated, the Crewe route alignment remained unaltered; it is the left track in the lower left corner of this 1908 map at 6ins to 1 mile. Curving away from it is the new position of the Chester tracks. The old line is shown as a siding down to the canal, where it connects with the waterside line of the MSC. The old and new junctions are marked; above them, the lines run north over the River Weaver. Our journey ends near the top of the map.

Manchester Ship Canal Bridge

85.   We look west under Acton Grange Viaduct in 1904. It had been completed in the previous year and came into use on 1st January 1904, when the canal opened. The elevated signal box was replaced by a flat-roofed type on 5th May 1940, south of the canal. It had 40 levers and was closed on 17th September 1972. The skew span had to be 233ft to provide a square span of 120ft. (A.Dudman coll.)

86.   The signal box was a wartime design, as was this 2-8-0, one of a large batch produced for the War Department. It is a post-1948 view, with assorted shabby wagons. (Bentley coll.)

87.   A better record of the bridge includes no. 48455, also an LMS class 8F 2-8-0 design, introduced in 1935. However, this was one of a batch built by the GWR in 1943-45, under Government direction. (Bentley coll.)

88.   The bridge and 1940 signal box are in the background as no. 46241 *City of Edinburgh* accelerates south. This is one of the "Princess Coronation" class 4-6-2s, introduced by the LMS in 1937. (G.Coltas Trust/Bentley coll.)

Walton Old Junction

89.   Running towards the canal bridge is 2-8-0 no. 48357, a class 8F of LMS origin. The line rising on the right is from Arpley. (Bentley coll.)

90.   The location is the same, although a little to the north of the previous view. An eleven coach up train was recorded in July 1965. (Bentley coll.)

91.   Between Arpley Junction and Walton Old Junction on 8th July 1965 is 0-6-0 no. 44181. This class 4F design was introduced by the LMS in 1924. (Bentley coll.)

92.   No. 90045 backs into Walton Old Junction Yard with the 10.45 Speedlink from Willesden. The traffic on this occasion has all been picked up at Crewe and comprises two empty ferry vans from Crewe to Lynemouth, one empty ferry flat to Dover and ten empty vans. The date is 25th June 1991. (P.D.Shannon)

93.   Nos 20113 and 20106 pass Walton Old Junction with the Speedlink feeder service from Trafford Park to Warrington Arpley. Class 20s were regular performers on this service during the final weeks of Speedlink. The photograph is from 27th June 1991. (P.D.Shannon)

British Rlys(M) For   British Rlys(M) For
conditions see back   conditions see back
THIRD CLASS   THIRD CLASS
SINGLE   SINGLE
Norton(Ches.   Norton(Ches.
Norton Ches.   To
WARRINGTON (BANK QUAY)
WarringtonBQ   WarringtonBQ
10 Z⁴ FARE 1/0 ∠

3596   3596

94.   By February 1992, class 60s had taken over all North West coal duties formerly entrusted to class 20s, with the exception of the Bickershaw branch drawback locomotives. No. 60069 approaches Walton Old Junction sidings with the 07.00 Silverdale - Fiddlers Ferry service on 4th January 1992. (P.D.Shannon)

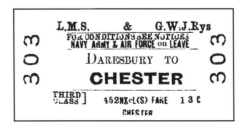

L.M.S.   &   G.W.J.Rys

303   303

FOR CONDITIONS SEE NOTICES
NAVY ARMY & AIR FORCE on LEAVE

DARESBURY TO

CHESTER

THIRD]
CLASS]   452NXcL(S) FARE   13 C

CHESTER

95.   At Walton Old Junction on 23rd October 2007 is no. 66619, with a coal train of bogie hoppers. Fiddlers Ferry power station would often demand almost 100,000 tons of coal per week. (P.D.Shannon)

96.   Reverting to 28th July 1982, we witness the earlier generation of coal hoppers on a merry-go-round service from Parkside to Fiddlers Ferry. The train has reversed at Warrington Old Bank and its locomotives (nos 20059 and 20068) are on the rear. No. 31200 will take the train forward to Latchford Sidings, where it will reverse again to run west to the power station. (T.Heavyside)

WARRINGTON BANK QUAY

97.   This northward view is from about 1925 and shows High Level, which came into use on 16th November 1868, when the previous station closed. It had been a little to the north and the original terminus at Dallam Lane was in use from June 1831 until July 1837. (Stations UK)

98.   Low Level is shown for completeness. It was open until 9th September 1963 and is pictured in around 1925. Local passenger services ceased on 10th September 1962, but two freight lines are still busy. (Stations UK)

99.   Entering in 1939 is no. 6160 *Queen Victoria's Rifleman*, one of the "Royal Scot" class 6P 4-6-0s. Judging by its length, the train is probably calling at all stations. The GWR sold 5513 tickets here in 1923. (Bentley coll.)

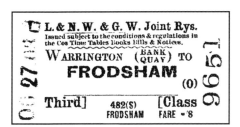

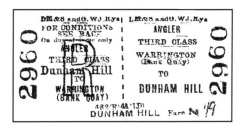

100.   Seen at the same time is a long distance train hauled by 4-6-0s nos. 5353 and 5385. Later rated 5MT, this class was not generally named. Tickets sold by the GWR numbered 2987 in 1938. (Bentley coll.)

101.   The main entrance was recorded in about 1955, when parcels by passenger train were handled at the doorway. (Milepost 92½)

102.   No. 2 Box had 82 levers and was in use from about 1925 until 17th September 1972. The photograph is from around 1960 and it includes the brick arches supporting Sankey Street. (Milepost 92½)

103.   Heading a down express on 3rd July 1964 is no. 46148 *The Girl Guide*, a "Royal Scot" class 4-6-0. Colour light signals have arrived. (G.Coltas Trust/Bentley coll.)

104.   No. 2 Box is seen on 26th November 1964, together with part of Joseph Crosfield's Soap Works which was started in 1914. It had sidings at the low level and became part of Unilever in 1929, ICI in 1997 and the PQ Corporation in 2008. (R.J.Essery/R.S.Carpenter)

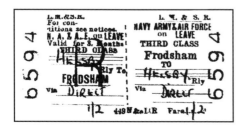

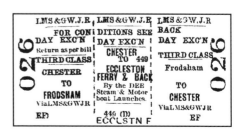

105. A panorama from June 1966 features BR 4-6-2 No. 70002 *Geoffrey Chaucer* arriving, having just passed over the Manchester Ship Canal. The three signals above the rear coach give drivers arriving from Chester the alternatives of two platforms or the through line. (H.C.Casserley)

106. We are looking south near No. 2 Box on 21st June 1966. Local services had been withdrawn thus: to Bolton (Great Moor Street) in 1954 and St. Helens (Shaw Street) in 1964. The latter had been push-pull operated. (H.C.Casserley)

107.   Seen on the same day, BR class 5MT 4-6-0 no. 73160 departs south with its drain cocks open. The locomotive and its environs were very shabby by that time. (H.C.Casserley)

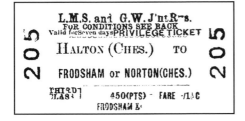

108.   Reversing a freight train on 29th August 1967 is "Black Five" 4-6-0 no. 45323, while the staff of No. 2 Box have the opportunity to observe it. (E.Wilmshurst)

→   109.   The lower windows are for the machine room, where the interlocking equipment is situated and maintained. Some of the point rodding emerges from below its floor and then runs under the rails. (E.Wilmshurst)

→   110. We look south on 25th April 1974, in an era when industrial black smoke and mounds of mailbags were common sights. The two vans in the short platform were probably for that traffic. The works also produced candles from an early date. (H.C.Casserley)

111. The short siding comes into view on 10th October 1981 and it becomes apparent that it had received overhead wiring. No. 47537 waits to depart with the 13.38 Bangor to Manchester service. (T.Heavyside)

➜ 112. The photographer stands in the dry as no. 87024 approaches platform 3, with a Euston to Glasgow express on 9th August 1982. (D.H.Mitchell)

➜ 113. Seen on the same day before the rain is no. 47405 hauling the 13.45 Manchester Victoria to Bangor as it enters platform 1. The line in the foreground gives direct access to the sidings near Warrington Old Junction. (D.H.Mitchell)

114.   No. 47195 is heading empty tankers bound for Stanlow on 28th October 1988. It will run via Helsby and is on the line on the right of the previous picture. The Power Signal Box of 1972 is on the right. Its flat roof had to be replaced in the early 1980s by a pitched one, owing to leakage. (T.Heavyside)

115.   On the right on the same day is no. 87006 with a down train, while no. 90011 waits with freight on the loop beyond platform 1. (T.Heavyside)

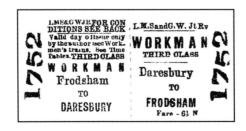

116.   No. 86430 arrives with the 08.30 Glasgow to Euston on 4th May 1989. The soap works is being extended further, but by that time it was producing a wide range of chemicals, especially for detergents and toothpaste. (A.C.Hartless)

→   117. A crew training train was recorded at platform 2 on 23rd March 1991. No. 158781 was running from Manchester to Chester. (T.Heavyside)

→   118. Leaving platform 4 on 10th April 2003 is no. 142009. The loop on the left was normally used by down freight trains. (P.D.Shannon)

119.   Platform lengthening was in progress in March 2011 when a "Pendolino" unit was recorded entering No. 2. Classified 390, this stock was introduced in 2004 and was admired for its tilting ability, but detested for its tiny windows. (Virgin Trains)

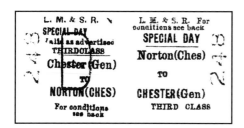

120.   No. 175113 is at platform 4 on 17th November 2012, working the 11.44 Llandudno to Manchester service. These popular "Coradia" units serve Warrington well, the station acting as one of the main crossroads in England's rail network. (H.Ballantyne)

MP Middleton Press

EVOLVING THE ULTIMATE RAIL ENCYCLOPEDIA

Easebourne Lane, Midhurst, West Sussex.
GU29 9AZ   Tel:01730 813169

www.middletonpress.co.uk   email:info@middletonpress.co.uk
A-978 0 906520   B- 978 1 873793   C- 978 1 901706   D-978 1 904474
F - 978 1 906008   F - 978 1 908174

All titles listed below were in print at time of publication - please check current availability by looking at our website - **www.middletonpress.co.uk** or by requesting a Brochure which includes our *LATEST* RAILWAY TITLES also our TRAMWAY, TROLLEYBUS, MILITARY and COASTAL series